W9-DGI-698

A Perspectives Flip Book

The Split History of

WORLD WAR I

ALLIES PERSPECTIVE

by Michael Burgan

Content Consultant:
Timothy Solie
Adjunct Professor
Department of History
Minnesota State University, Mankato

COMPASS POINT BOOKS
a capstone imprint

Compass Point Books are published by Capstone,
1710 Roe Crest Drive, North Mankato, Minnesota 56003
www.capstonepub.com

Library of Congress Cataloging-in-Publication Data
Burgan, Michael.
  The split history of World War I: a perspectives flip book / by Michael Burgan.
     pages cm. — (Perspectives flip books)
  Includes bibliographical references and index.
  Summary: "Describes the opposing viewpoints of the Allies and the Central Powers during
  World War I"—Provided by publisher.
  ISBN 978-0-7565-4694-6 (library binding)
  ISBN 978-0-7565-4700-4 (paperback)
  ISBN 978-0-7565-4702-8 (ebook PDF)
  ISBN 978-0-7565-4704-2 (reflowable epub)
  1. World War, 1914–1918—Juvenile literature. I. Title. II. Title: Split history of World War One.
   D522.7.B87 2014
   940.3—dc23   2013007019

MANAGING EDITOR
CATHERINE NEITGE

LIBRARY CONSULTANT
KATHLEEN BAXTER

DESIGNERS
GENE BENTDAHL AND SARAH BENNETT

PRODUCTION SPECIALIST
LAURA MANTHE

MEDIA RESEARCHER
WANDA WINCH

IMAGE CREDITS

Allies Perspective: "The American soldiers in the presence of gas, 42nd Div., Essey, France."
Sept. 20, 1918. (Reeve #037283) OHA 80: Reeve Photograph Collection. Otis Historical
Archives, National Museum of Health & Medicine, cover (top); Capstone, 13; Corbis: Leonard
de Selva, 5; CRIAimages.com: Jay Robert Nash Collection, 6, 14, 28; Library of Congress: Prints
and Photographs Division, cover (bottom), 10, 17, 19, 21, 23; National Archives and Records
Administration, 25, 26

Central Powers Perspective: "The American soldiers in the presence of gas, 42nd Div., Essey,
France." Sept. 20, 1918. (Reeve #037283) OHA 80: Reeve Photograph Collection. Otis Historical
Archives, National Museum of Health & Medicine, cover (bottom); Corbis, 26, adoc-photos, 27,
Hulton-Deutsch Collection, 23; CRIAImages.com: Jay Robert Nash Collection, 12, 15, 17, 18, 24,
29; Getty Images Inc: Keystone, 11, Time Life Pictures/Mansell, 5; Library of Congress: Prints and
Photographs Division, cover (top), 8, 20

Art elements: Shutterstock: Color Symphony, paper texture, Ebtikar, flag, Sandra Cunningham,
grunge photo, SvetlanaR, grunge lines

Printed in the United States of America in North Mankato, Minnesota.

032013   007223CGF13

Table of
Contents

THE GREAT WAR BEGINS

*I*n his office in London, Sir Edward Grey opened the first of several telegrams that would soon shock the world. It was June 28, 1914. Grey was the foreign secretary of Great Britain. He read the news that Archduke Franz Ferdinand, who was next in line to rule the Austro-Hungarian Empire, had been shot and killed in Sarajevo, the capital of Bosnia and Herzegovina. Grey knew that the assassination could lead to a huge conflict—for Britain and the rest of the world.

The killer, Gavrilo Princip, was a Bosnian Serb with close ties to the military of Serbia. He supported Serbia's desire that Bosnia and Herzegovina become independent from Austria-Hungary.

A 1914 Paris newspaper illustration depicts Gavrilo Princip firing the fatal shots.

Russia's leader, Tsar Nicholas II, supported Serbia in its aim to weaken Austria-Hungary in that part of Europe, known as the Balkans.

Britain had long tried to remain independent from the other major European powers. It focused more on building an overseas empire. But since the 1870s, nations with shared interests had formed alliances. Austria-Hungary, Italy, and Germany created one of these alliances. France and Russia, worried about the growing economic and military strength of Germany, formed another. Great Britain joined France and Russia in 1907 to create the Triple Entente.

For weeks after the assassination, Grey and other leaders in Europe waited to see if Austria-Hungary would respond with a military strike. They worried such an attack could spark a much larger war.

Austria-Hungary sent a list of 12 demands to the Serbian government on July 23. The Serbs accepted all but two — demands that would virtually end their independence and give Austria-Hungary control over their affairs. The Serbs then reached out to Russia, which promised to help them fight a war. Germany had already promised Austria-Hungary it would enter the war if Russia did.

Three days later Grey tried to organize a conference of European ambassadors to stop the threat of a large-scale war. The idea went nowhere. Grey told a German official that if war began, "it will be the greatest catastrophe that the world has ever seen."

Austria-Hungary fired on Serbia on July 29. They were the first shots of what would come to be called the Great War. Soon the fighting spread north, as German troops moved through Belgium and Luxembourg on their way to France.

Belgium and Luxembourg were neutral, although both had good relations with Britain and France. The British had promised to help defend Belgium if Germany attacked. On August 4 Great Britain declared war on Germany, and eight days later it declared war on Austria-Hungary. Joining the British were its dominions of Canada,

Belgian soldiers march to war in 1914.

Australia, New Zealand, and South Africa and its colonies. The British said they were fighting to protect independence and other values that were "vital to the civilized world." Britain also wanted to keep Germany's power under control.

Germany and Austria-Hungary would later get help from Bulgaria and the Ottoman Empire, which was based in what is now Turkey. Germany was the main military power of this group, called the Central Powers.

In the Triple Entente, Russia and France had the largest armies, while Britain had a powerful navy. Soon after declaring war, Britain sent a small land force to help France fight the Germans. Several million more troops would follow in the months and years to come. But in the first weeks of the war, the French and Belgians did most of the fighting against Germany.

For the French, the war was about defending itself from a German attack. But France also wanted to regain Alsace-Lorraine, a region to its northeast it had lost to Germany after an earlier war.

France counted heavily on Russia's help. Together with Great Britain, France and Russia were now known as the Allies.

THE TWO FRONTS

France attacked the Germans in Alsace-Lorraine, but most of the heavy fighting took place farther north in France and Belgium. The British Army's first major action took place at Mons, Belgium, in August. Despite being outnumbered more than two to one, the British fought so well that the German commander thought they were using machine guns instead of rifles. But the larger German forces gained the upper hand and forced the British to retreat. German troops then continued their advance on Paris, the capital of France. By September French casualties were more than 260,000. Along the Marne River, the Allies stopped the invading enemy, who began to retreat September 9. Several thousand French reinforcements had piled into 600 taxicabs in Paris to reach the battle.

In October some of the heaviest fighting took place near the Belgian city of Ypres. The Germans managed to take some land, but the Allies remained in the region. They were determined to keep all the territory they held, even though they were paying a high cost in casualties.

Russia's army was the world's largest with 1.4 million troops, but it had trouble against the Central Powers. The Russians had had some success in Galicia, which was part of Austria-Hungary. But they had then suffered a major defeat against the Germans at the Battle of Tannenberg at the end of August. Over the next several months, the Russians continued to fight with no major victories. As 1914 ended the Allies realized they faced a long war against a determined enemy.

YEARS OF DESTRUCTION

CH 2

Troops moved freely across the battlefield in the war's early months. But by 1915 the war centered on trenches on the Western Front, a line stretching more than 450 miles (725 kilometers) across northern France between the Swiss border and the North Sea. The men lived in the trenches and used them for protection from enemy attacks. The land between Allied trenches and the enemy's was known as no man's land. British trenches were about 7 feet (2 meters) deep and 6 feet (1.8 m) wide, although the sizes varied. As fighting moved from one area to another, the soldiers built more connecting trenches, creating complicated mazes.

An abandoned British trench, which was captured by the Germans

British soldier Arthur Maitland wrote his parents that he stayed in the trenches almost all the time. The Germans "shell us constantly but we laugh at them from our burrows like rabbits." But a fellow soldier, Neville Woodroffe, wrote home about the huge number of deaths he saw and said, "This is a terrible war." He was killed a month later.

Even as the Allies tried to kill the Germans, the two sides did at times realize their enemies were human. In December 1914 British and German soldiers in parts of France and Belgium shared what was called the Christmas truce. They stopped fighting for the holiday. They sang Christmas carols, and German soldiers set up Christmas trees. Enemy troops even came out of the trenches to shake hands with each other. But after Christmas was over, the soldiers once again returned to the war, determined to beat their enemies.

BATTLES BEYOND EUROPE

The Great War soon spread beyond land. With its powerful navy, the British formed a blockade against Germany. The British stopped ships that were delivering supplies to its enemy. They seized any materials they thought might help the Germans, including food and cloth.

Many European nations had colonies in Africa and Asia, and fierce fighting went on in those places as well. In the Pacific Ocean, troops from Australia and New Zealand seized German-controlled islands. Japan had joined the Allied cause in August 1914. British soldiers helped Japanese troops take Tsingtao, a city in China that Germany controlled. In Africa battles took place in what is now Tanzania and Namibia. Both the British and French also used residents of their colonies to fight in Europe. Although not called a world war at the time, the Great War was truly worldwide.

Some of the major fighting in Asia took place on the western edge of the continent. When the Ottoman Empire, based in present-day Turkey, joined the Central Powers, British military leaders wanted to take the battle to the Turks. British troops eventually fought across the Middle East, which was then mostly part of the Ottoman Empire. Allied troops planned to invade the region at the Gallipoli Peninsula on the European side of the Dardanelles, a narrow strait that divides Europe and Asia. The Allies knew if they controlled the Dardanelles, they could push forward to the Ottoman capital, Constantinople (now called Istanbul).

The first of about 70,000 Allied forces came ashore at the Gallipoli Peninsula starting April 25, 1915. Many of the troops were from Australia and New Zealand. In the months to come, those forces faced heavy losses as they tried to push out the Ottoman troops. A major offensive failed in August. One New Zealander, Charlie Clark, later described hearing "thump, thump, thump and it was fellows falling around me. Nine or ten of them, suddenly wounded or dead …" The Allies pulled out their troops early in 1916. The Dardanelles invasion was a daring military move that ended badly. But it did keep Turkish troops from fighting the Russians.

FIGHTING BACK IN EUROPE

The Dardanelles campaign lasted almost a year. During that time fighting continued on the Western Front, though neither side made major gains. The two sides had clashed near Ypres, Belgium, in April 1915. This time French troops faced a new danger—chlorine, a gas that is poisonous in large amounts. German soldiers opened steel tanks to release the gas, which drifted over French troops in their trenches. One French soldier described his reaction to the gas attack: "It burned my throat, caused pains in my chest and made breathing all but impossible. I spat blood and suffered dizziness. We all thought that we were lost."

The Allies fought back by developing gas masks to protect their soldiers and shells that could fire gas at the Germans. But gas warfare did not always work as planned. At the Battle of Loos in autumn 1915, British troops watched in horror as gas aimed at

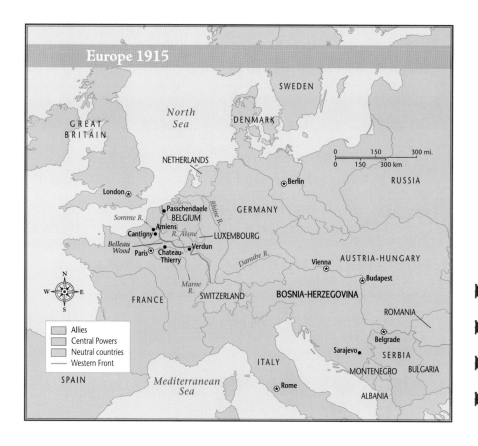

Europe 1915

SWEDEN

North Sea

DENMARK

GREAT BRITAIN

NETHERLANDS

London ⊗

Berlin ⊗

RUSSIA

Passchendaele
BELGIUM
Somme R.
Amiens
Cantigny
R. Aisne — LUXEMBOURG
Belleau Wood
Paris ⊗
Verdun
Chateau-Thierry

GERMANY

Rhine R.

Danube R.

Vienna ⊗

AUSTRIA-HUNGARY

Budapest ⊗

Marne R.

FRANCE

SWITZERLAND

BOSNIA-HERZEGOVINA

ROMANIA

Belgrade ⊗

Sarajevo •

SERBIA

ITALY

MONTENEGRO

BULGARIA

SPAIN

Mediterranean Sea

Rome ⊗

ALBANIA

0   150   300 mi.
0   150   300 km

Allies
Central Powers
Neutral countries
Western Front

the Germans drifted back toward them. The gas injured more than 2,600 British soldiers and seven died.

On the Eastern Front, which covered Russia, Germany, and Austria-Hungary, Russia continued to suffer against its enemies in 1915. The Allies also saw Serbia finally fall to the Central Powers, after it had resisted several invasions. During 1915 the fighting also spread to Italy, which had joined the Allies. In a secret deal, the Allies offered to give some Austrian territory to Italy if it helped fight the Central Powers. But Italian soldiers struggled when battling Austro-Hungarian troops near the Alps between Austria and Italy.

MAJOR BATTLES OF 1916

As 1916 began the French could see German activity near the city of Verdun, France. Several forts surrounded the city. After losing Fort Duoaumont at the end of February, the French could have pulled back. Instead General Philippe Pétain was determined to fight for Verdun. His artillery fired on the German troops, and French fighter planes took to the skies. They shot down German planes and fired rockets at German balloons. A road leading into Verdun saw a constant stream of French trucks bringing food, supplies, and more soldiers to the city.

French troops take cover during the Battle of Verdun.

NEW WAY OF FIGHTING

In 1915 the British began working on a new weapon, the tank. The British designed a war vehicle with armor to protect troops inside, a gun, and metal treads that would let it roll over trenches. The first British tank, the Mark I, entered battle in September 1916. By the end of the war, the Allies had built several thousand tanks. The most commonly used model, the FT 17, came from France. The Germans had trouble building tanks that performed as well as the Allied tanks. German soldiers sometimes used captured Allied tanks instead.

Through the rest of the year, the two sides battled for control of Verdun. The French took back land the Germans had won earlier. When the fighting finally ended, the Germans saw how hard it was to push out well-supplied French forces fighting in their own country. They would not launch another major offensive until 1918. But the French paid a high price, with about 400,000 casualties.

To draw away German troops from France, Russia launched a daring new offensive in the east. General Alexei Brusilov commanded the attack. Starting in June his troops rolled through the Austro-Hungarian forces, who were surprised by the attack. They thought the system of trenches they had dug, some up to 20 feet (6 m) deep, would keep the Russians away. Instead, as Russian troops quickly moved forward, the Austrians became trapped in the trenches. The Russians captured about 400,000 prisoners before Central Powers' reinforcements slowed their advance. The Brusilov Offensive showed the Russians at their best on the battlefield. But it also cost them almost 500,000 casualties.

The third major campaign of 1916 came in the west, along France's Somme River. This time the British led the way, under the command of General Douglas Haig. The Battle of the Somme turned into a bloody, ugly struggle. The British were counting on their artillery to clear out front-line German troops in late June. Then British soldiers would move forward to fight the remaining soldiers. But the British didn't have enough guns and shells to destroy German artillery. Meanwhile, the Germans had time to set up their machine guns and fire on the British soldiers. In just the first day, July 1, the British suffered nearly 60,000 casualties, including nearly 20,000 dead. Soldiers carried off the wounded using whatever they could find, including wheelbarrows and wooden planks. After that brutal day, both sides launched small offensives, without major gains.

In September British tanks rolled through battlefields for the first time. Many broke down or were destroyed, but they did help the British make some gains. Heavy rainfall in October turned the battlefield into a sea of mud and hampered progress by either army. The German Army retreated in November, but it wasn't a victory for the Allies, who had suffered more than 600,000 casualties. About two-thirds of those were British.

THE HOME FRONT

At the start of the war, Great Britain relied on volunteers for its military. But by 1916 it was drafting young men to join the army. The other Allies were already using a draft. Some people in Britain were pacifists, meaning they opposed all war. The government did

French women work in the fields without horses. Retreating German soldiers took the animals with them.

allow men to avoid fighting if they had religious or moral reasons for opposing the war. But some of the men who refused to fight were tried and sent to prison.

In all the Allied nations, civilians faced food shortages, and food was often rationed. People could buy only limited amounts of sugar, meat, and dairy products. In England the government took control of the railroads and raised taxes for the war effort. Cities and towns used parkland to raise crops.

Women played a large role on the home front. They went to work in factories to build weapons or plow fields once farmed by men. Some British women learned how to defend themselves and their families as part of the Women's Defence Relief Corps. The women were also trained to replace men in factories so the men could join the military. Women also got close to battle, serving as nurses. Some did more than help the wounded. Edith Cavell was a British nurse living in Belgium when the war broke out. She helped Allied troops escape Belgium. The Germans arrested and killed her for her actions. Another British woman, Flora Sandes, went to Serbia when the war began and fought for that country.

CHANGING FORCES

W hile the war waged in Europe, Americans closely followed the action. Millions of immigrants had come from countries now battling each other. Tens of thousands had already returned to Europe to help defend their homelands. U.S. businesses shipped goods to the Allies. The United States was technically neutral, but President Woodrow Wilson and many Americans favored close ties with Great Britain. The two countries had strong business relations as well as a shared language.

A 1915 British army recruitment poster

An incident in May 1915 increased American anger with Germany. The British passenger ship *Lusitania* was sailing from New York to England. Along with almost 2,000 people, the ship carried war supplies for the British. On May 7 a German submarine fired a torpedo at the ship off the coast of Ireland. American citizen Michael Byrne later described hearing "a thunderous roar, as if the skies opened" when the torpedo exploded. As the lifeboats near him quickly filled, Byrne jumped into the water and began swimming until another lifeboat rescued him. Byrne was lucky. The German attack sank the *Lusitania* and killed nearly 1,200 people, including 128 Americans.

Across Great Britain and the United States, people criticized the deadly German attack. Former U.S. president Theodore Roosevelt called it a "vaster scale of murder than old-time pirates ever practiced." U.S. President Woodrow Wilson demanded that Germany admit that the killing of neutral American passengers was illegal. Germany refused. In September 1915, though, it did agree to attack only armed merchant ships or warships.

WILSON REACHES A LIMIT

Wilson tried to get the Allies and Central Powers to discuss peace at the beginning of 1916. That effort failed, but the Germans did agree to stop attacking armed merchant ships without warning. As the war dragged on, though, Germany changed its mind. In January 1917 it once again vowed to attack any ships off British waters without warning. Wilson cut off diplomatic relations with Germany on February 3.

Wilson's anti-German feelings increased in late February after he learned about an earlier German offer to Mexico. The British intercepted a coded telegram sent in January by a German official to the German ambassador to Mexico. The telegram said that in case the U.S. joined the Allies, "we make Mexico a proposal of alliance on the following basis: make war together, make peace together, generous financial support and an understanding on our part that Mexico is to reconquer the lost territory in Texas, New Mexico, and Arizona."

Wilson asked Congress to declare war on April 2, saying, "The world must be made safe for democracy." Congress voted to do so four days later. U.S. troops began preparing for war.

At first the United States' decision didn't change much on the battlefield. The Allies launched the Nivelle Offensive in April 1917 in central France, which they hoped would end the war within two days with few casualties. But French casualties alone were about 40,000 in just one day, and the army gained almost no land. Some French soldiers, tired of war and so many losses, refused to fight. General Pétain, who replaced Nivelle, increased soldiers' leave to help morale.

British soldiers drag a small cannon through the mud.

In July another battle began outside Ypres, with the British leading the attack. General Haig fought on even as rain created huge fields of mud. His men showed signs of losing their fighting spirit. One British soldier later wrote, "If you got hit, the chances were you slipped into some yawning shell-hole full of greyly opaque water concealing unmentionable things and you drowned there." The British did manage to gain a small bit of land in the three-month battle, but at the cost of more than 300,000 casualties.

In the east Russia had gone through a revolution. Tsar Nicholas II was imprisoned and a new government now controlled the military. The Russians launched a new offensive in July, but the Germans soon counterattacked and scored several victories.

By fall the new Russian government was under assault from its own people. Russian socialists called Bolsheviks, who wanted government ownership of farms and factories, came to power. Led by Vladimir Lenin, the Bolsheviks asked the Germans for peace. The Allies lost one of their major militaries and were angry that the Russians had abandoned them. Allied leaders also feared that the

Bolsheviks would try to spread socialism in Europe. With Russia out of the war, the Germans were free to move many troops from the Eastern Front to the west.

HEADING TO EUROPE

The first U.S. forces reached France in June 1917, under the command of General John "Black Jack" Pershing. They were met by cheering crowds who believed the Americans would help the Allies win the war.

Germany had now increased its submarine war, and ships crossing the Atlantic with U.S. troops and supplies were favored targets. To fight back the Allies used convoys—large groups of ships defended by naval vessels. By July 1917 several dozen U.S. warships were based in Europe, helping with the convoys.

As in other Allied countries, war changed daily life for many Americans. The U.S. government created propaganda to stir up hatred for the Central Powers, especially Germany. Support for the war was not particularly strong. Many Americans had ties to Germany, and most Irish Americans disliked the British, since they had treated the Irish badly in their homeland. Some Americans were pacifists or socialists who opposed the war.

The propaganda against Germany sometimes made life hard for German-Americans. In some places local governments no longer allowed schools to teach the German language, and musicians refused to play German music. A few German-Americans were beaten or even killed for alleged disloyalty to the United States.

As in Europe, the U.S. government took control of parts of the economy to help the war effort. The War Industries Board directed companies to make supplies for the military. The Food Administration encouraged Americans to grow more of their own food so farmers' crops could go to the troops. The National War Labor Board kept good relations between companies and workers, so the workers would not strike. Large strikes were a problem for the French and British.

American gardeners were urged to back the war effort.

The war led to other changes in the United States. As in Europe, women began to work in factories. Large numbers of African-Americans moved off southern farms to work in northern cities. They were part of a "Great Migration" that saw about 500,000 blacks leave the South during the war. And while the war stopped most immigration to the United States from Europe, nearly 900,000 Mexicans entered the country between 1910 and 1920.

Through 1917 Americans at home mobilized for war as U.S. troops trained in Europe and took part in several battles. The next year they would finally fight in large numbers on the battlefields of France.

CH. 4 PEACE AT LAST

The Allies faced heavy losses, particularly on the Western

Front, through 1917. The Central Powers, though, were losing their

will to fight. German leaders no longer expected to win the war,

but they wanted to launch several last major offensives and grab as

much land as possible.

The first offensive came in March 1918 along the Somme. The

British were forced to give back land they had won at the battle

there in 1916. Large German guns began to shell Paris. But starting

in May, American troops began to play a role in stopping the

German advance. They won a battle at Cantigny, and in June

American soldiers on the front line in France

helped the Allies win the Battle of Belleau Wood. Though they lacked training, the Americans fought hard, leading Australian officer Edwin Trundle to write, "I'm sure the Yanks are going to prove excellent fighting troops."

A FINAL PUSH

The Allies began several major counterattacks in July, starting along the Marne River and then in Amiens. By the end of August, American General Pershing was planning to use his forces against the Germans near the town of St. Mihiel. But Marshal Ferdinand Foch of France, who was in charge of the other Allied forces, had different ideas. He wanted to move some of the Americans to other locations. The two commanders began to argue, with Foch asking if Pershing wanted to go to battle. "Most assuredly," Pershing replied, "but as an American army."

Foch finally agreed to keep the Americans together. They fought at St. Mihiel. In late September they moved north to the Argonne Forest. There and along the Meuse River, the Americans faced their

An American gun crew attacks the German position.

toughest fighting of the war. More than 26,000 soldiers were killed and 95,000 wounded in the fighting, which lasted into November.

James "Slim" Jones fought in that campaign. He later recalled how he and just six other men attacked a German machine gun position "with all pistols blazing … we got 132 prisoners and captured nine machine guns."

The Allied successes during the fall convinced British and French military leaders that the war would soon be over. But the Germans refused to give up. As the Germans pulled back to a defensive position known as the Hindenburg Line, British artillery rained shells on them. By late September the Allies had broken through the line. At almost the same time, Bulgaria agreed to stop fighting in the Balkans. It was the first of the Central Powers to seek peace.

Meanwhile, the British were gaining ground against the Ottoman Empire in the Middle East. In the Alps between Italy and Austria, the Italians now greatly outnumbered their weakened enemy. October fighting along the Piave River led to an Italian victory. German leaders were finally ready to discuss ending the war.

THE 14 POINTS

In January 1918 President Wilson had proposed 14 Points that he thought should shape the peace process. Wilson wanted to end the Great War in a way that would lead to lasting peace and spread democracy across Europe. His points included the return of French land from Germany, including Alsace-Lorraine; independence for the various ethnic groups in Austria-Hungary and the Ottoman Empire; a free Poland; and an international organization that would protect each nation's independence and work to prevent future wars. As for Germany, Wilson said, "We do not wish to injure her or to block in any way her legitimate influence or power."

The fighting stopped November 11, 1918—at the 11th hour of the 11th day of the 11th month. People celebrated the armistice across Europe. A U.S. soldier in Paris, George Alexander, described the scene: "Paris went wild in about two minutes. People flocked out into the streets—until it was almost impossible to drive thru … Well—we shipped our baggage on … and went crazy with the rest of Paris. Never before in my life was I hugged—kissed—and pushed about—as much."

Germany agreed to give up most of its military equipment and release prisoners of war. Meanwhile, the Allied blockade continued as the two sides discussed peace. The Allies, though, didn't allow Germany to attend the peace conference that began in Paris in January 1919. The Allies would decide the terms of peace—and Germany would have to accept them.

The peace conference showed strong differences among the Allies. Wilson was determined to keep his 14 Points at the center of

The leaders who shaped the Versailles Treaty (from left, seated): Vittorio Orlando of Italy, David Lloyd George of Great Britain, Georges Clemenceau of France, and Woodrow Wilson of the United States.

the discussion. But British Prime Minister David Lloyd George and French Premier Georges Clemenceau wanted to punish Germany as much as possible. While Wilson had called for creating several new independent states, the other Allies had already signed secret treaties that divided up lands in the Ottoman Empire and former German colonies. But a number of independent countries did emerge in Europe, including Finland, Poland, Czechoslovakia, and Yugoslavia.

The Allies also argued over reparations. Britain and France wanted Germany to pay a high price. To Wilson, excessive reparations would give Germany "powerful reasons for wishing one day to take revenge." But Wilson was willing to go along with reparations and other British and French demands, as long as the peace treaty created the new international organization he sought. The Treaty of Versailles did call for a League of Nations.

The final peace treaty forced Germany to give up land, greatly reduce the size of its military, and take blame for starting the Great War. Many of the new countries formed in Europe came out of the Austro-Hungarian Empire. Italy also gained land from the Austrians, and France took control of western Germany.

Not everyone was happy with the final agreement. Marshal Ferdinand Foch of France said the treaty the Allies and Germans signed was not peace, it was "an armistice for 20 years." Foch thought another huge war was bound to erupt in Europe. And he was right.

Some U.S. lawmakers disliked the treaty, especially the part about the League of Nations. They didn't want the United States dragged into future European wars. The country hadn't suffered as much as France or Great Britain. Still, in just six months of major combat, about 50,000 Americans had been killed in battle. More than that died of disease. A worldwide flu epidemic that spread among the troops killed both soldiers and citizens. And like the soldiers of other countries, thousands of Americans had come home "shell-shocked." Their mental health suffered because of the horrible things they had experienced in Europe. Today this condition is called post-traumatic stress disorder.

In the end, dozens of nations joined the League of Nations. But the United States was not one of them. The league could not prevent another European war—a war started in 1939 by Germany. World War I had left Germany weak, and many Germans wanted to rebuild their military and once again show their strength. World War II had many causes—one of them was the harsh peace the Allies called for after World War I.

INDEX

INTERNET SITES

Use FactHound to find Internet sites related to this book. All of the sites on FactHound have been researched by our staff.

Here's all you do:
Visit *www.facthound.com*
Type in this code: 9780756545727

-1-

GLOSSARY

ALLIANCE—an agreement between nations or groups of people to work together

ARMISTICE—a formal agreement to end the fighting during a war

ARTILLERY—cannons and other large guns that fire explosives over long distances

ASSASSINATION—the murder of someone who is well known or important

BALKANS—countries on the Balkan Peninsula in southeastern Europe

CASUALTIES—soldiers killed, captured, missing, or injured during a war

ENTENTE—a French word meaning understanding, often used to describe the relationship between nations that agree to help each other

NEUTRAL—not supporting one side or the other in an argument or war

PROPAGANDA—information spread to try to influence the thinking of people; often not completely true or fair

SABOTAGE—damage or destruction that is done on purpose

STRIKE—to refuse to work because of a disagreement with the employer over wages or working conditions

WAR OF ATTRITION—fighting in which each side tries to wear down the other, rather than seeking to gain large areas of land

TIMELINE

1914

June 28: Archduke Franz Ferdinand of Austria-Hungary is assassinated in Sarajevo, Bosnia and Herzegovina

July 28: Austria-Hungary declares war on Serbia

August 1: Germany declares war on Russia; soon most major European nations join the fighting, with France and Great Britain aiding Russia and Serbia

August: Germany advances through Luxembourg and Belgium into France; Germany defeats Russia at the Battle of Tannenberg

September 5: The Battle of the Marne begins

1915

February: Germany declares the waters around Great Britain a war zone

April: German troops at Ypres, Belgium, use poison gas on the Allies

1917

January: Germany again decides to attack any ships entering British waters

April 6: The U.S. declares war on Germany

June: First U.S. forces reach France

July: The British suffer heavy casualties during the third Battle of Ypres

November: Bolsheviks take control of the Russian government and sign an armistice with Germany in December

1918

January: U.S. President Woodrow Wilson lists 14 Points that he hopes will shape the peace process when the war ends

March: Germany begins the first of a series of offensives along the Western Front

April 25: Allied forces land at Gallipoli Peninsula, Turkey

May 7: A German U-boat sinks the passenger ship *Lusitania*, killing almost 1,200 people

May 23: Italy declares war on Austria-Hungary

1916

February 21: The Germans launch a major offensive around the French city of Verdun

May 31: British and German naval ships fight their last major battle of the war, near Jutland, Denmark

June: The Russians' Brusilov Offensive leads to solid gains in the east, until Central Powers reinforcements stop them

July 1: The main part of the Battle of the Somme begins

May–June: U.S. troops have their first notable successes on the battlefield

September: The Allies break through Germany's last major defensive line; Bulgaria seeks peace with the Allies

November 9: Kaiser Wilhelm II announces he will step down

1919

November 11: The Allies and Central Powers agree to an armistice

January: The Allies begin working on the terms of a peace treaty

June 28: The Treaty of Versailles is signed

Select Bibliography

Chambers, John Whiteclay, II, ed. *The Oxford Companion to American Military History*. New York: Oxford University Press, 1999.

Davis, Belinda J. *Home Fires Burning: Food, Politics, and Everyday Life in World War I Berlin*. Chapel Hill: University of North Carolina Press, 2000.

Fleming, Thomas J. *The Illusion of Victory: America in World War I*. New York: Basic Books, 2004.

Hart, Peter. *The Somme: The Darkest Hour on the Western Front*. New York: Pegasus Books, 2010.

Herwig, Holger H. *The First World War: Germany and Austria–Hungary, 1914–1918*. New York: St. Martin's Press, 1997.

Keegan, John. *The First World War*. New York: A. Knopf, 1999.

Nelson, James Carl. *The Remains of Company D: A Story of the Great War*. New York: St. Martin's Press, 2009.

Paterson, Thomas G., et al. *American Foreign Relations: A History*. Vol. 2. Boston: Houghton Mifflin Co., 2005.

Strachan, Hew. *The First World War*. New York: Viking, 2004.

The Times Documentary History of the War. London: The Times Pub. Co., 1917.

Vansittart, Peter. *Voices from the Great War*. New York: Watts, 1984.

Willmott, H.P. *World War I*. New York: DK Pub., 2003.

Further Reading

Barber, Nicola. *World War I*. Chicago.: Heinemann Library, 2012.

Gregory, Josh. *World War I*. New York: Children's Press, 2012.

Heinrichs, Ann. *Voices of World War I: Stories from the Trenches*. Mankato, Minn.: Capstone Press, 2011.

Kent, Zachary: *World War I: From the Lusitania to Versailles*. Berkeley Heights, N.J.: Enslow Publishers, 2011.

Langley, Andrew. *The Hundred Days Offensive: The Allies' Push to Win World War I*. Minneapolis: Compass Point Books, 2009.

Slavicek, Louise Chipley. *The Treaty of Versailles*. New York: Chelsea House Publishers, 2010.

A Perspectives Flip Book

The Split History of

World War I

Central Powers Perspective

by Michael Burgan

Content Consultant:
Timothy Solie
Adjunct Professor
Department of History
Minnesota State University, Mankato

COMPASS POINT BOOKS
a capstone imprint

ABOUT THE AUTHOR:

Michael Burgan has written numerous books for children and young adults during his nearly 20 years as a freelance writer. Many of his books have focused on history, geography, and the lives of world leaders. Michael has won several awards for his writing. He lives in Santa Fe, New Mexico, with his cat, Callie.

SOURCE NOTES:

Allies Perspective

Page 6, line 5: Hew Strachan. *The First World War*. New York: Viking, 2004. p. 21.

Page 7, line 3: Peter Vansittart. *Voices from the Great War*. New York: Watts, 1984. p. 22.

Page 10, line 2: H.P. Willmott. *World War I*. New York: DK Pub., 2003. p. 56.

Page 10, line 5: Ibid. p. 61.

Page 11, line 6: The August Offensive, the Gallipoli Campaign. New Zealand History Online. 21 May 2013. http://www.nzhistory.net.nz/war/the-gallipoli-campaign/the-august-offensive

Page 12, line 19: Major Thomas S. Bundi, U.S. Army, PhD. "Gas, Mud, and Blood at Ypres: The Painful Lessons of Chemical Warfare." *Military Review*. July–August 2004. The Air University. 21 May 2013. http://www.au.af.mil/au/awc/awcgate/milreview/bundi.pdf

Page 19, line 16: The Lusitania Resource. 21 May 2013. http://www.rmslusitania.info/people/saloon/michael-byrne/

Page 19, line 23: Thomas G. Paterson, et al. *American Foreign Relations: A History*. Vol. 2. Boston: Houghton Mifflin Co., 2005. p. 270.

Page 20, line 12: The National Archives. 21 May 2013. http://www.archives.gov/global-pages/larger-image.html?i=/education/lessons/zimmermann/images/decoded-message-1.jpg&c=/education/lessons/zimmermann/images/decoded-message-caption.html

Page 20, line 16: Wilson's War Message to Congress. World War I Document Archive. 21 May 2013. http://wwi.lib.byu.edu/index.php/Wilson%27s_War_Message_to_Congress

Page 21, line 4: *World War I*. p. 20.

Page 25, line 3: Ibid. p. 220.

Page 25, line 12: "Disclose Pershing's Argument With Foch: Official Document of War Department Tells How American Commander Preserved Identity of A.E. F. as Unit in France." *The Pittsburgh Press*. 9 May 1929. 11 April 2013. http://news.google.com/newspapers?nid=1144&dat=19290509&id=PtbAAAAIBAJ&sjid=BUsEAAAAI BAJ&pg=4317,4124458

Page 26, line 3: James Carl Nelson. *The Remains of Company D: A Story of the Great War*. New York: St. Martin's Press, 2009. p. 283.

Page 27, line 9: President Wilson's Fourteen Points. The Avalon Project: Documents in Law, History and Diplomacy. 21 May 2013. http://avalon.law.yale.edu/20th_century/wilson14.asp

Page 27, line 14: In Their Own Words: Diaries, Memoirs, and Letters of the Past: Diary of George Ludovic Alexander. 21 May 2013. http://www.webmousepublications.com/itow/gla-1118.html

Page 28, line 10: *American Foreign Relations: A History*. Vol. 2. p. 92.

Page 29, line 8: *Voices from the Great War*. p. 263.

Central Powers Perspective:

Page 5, line 13: Autograph Letter of Franz Joseph to the Kaiser. World War I Document Archive. 21 May 2013. http://wwi.lib.byu.edu/index.php/Autograph_Letter_of_Franz_Joseph_to_the_Kaiser

Page 9, line 15: An eye-witness at Louvain. (1914) The History Collection. 21 May 2013. http://digicoll.library.wisc.edu/cgi-bin/History/History-idx?type=turn&entity=History.Louvain.p0005&id=History.Louvain&isize=M

Page 12, line 2: Annika Mombauer. *Helmuth von Moltke and the Origins of the First World War*. Cambridge: Cambridge University Press, 2001. p. 288.

Page 16, line 4: *World War I*. p. 135.

Page 19, line 18: Peter Hart. *The Somme: The Darkest Hour on the Western Front*. New York: Pegasus Books, 2010. p. 93.

Table of Contents

MURDER
CH. 1
SPARKS A WAR

Crowds cheered as Archduke Franz Ferdinand and his wife, Sophie, rode in an open car through the streets of Sarajevo, the capital of Bosnia and Herzegovina. The archduke was next in line to become emperor of Austria-Hungary. The empire stretched across Central Europe and into the southern part of the continent, called the Balkans.

Suddenly two shots rang out. The first shot passed through the side of the car, hitting the archduchess. The second shot killed Franz Ferdinand, who died calling for his wife. But Sophie was already dead. It was June 28, 1914, and in a month the world would be at war.

Angry Austrian officials immediately blamed Serbia, a neighbor

Archduke Franz Ferdinand and his wife, Sophie, moments before their deaths

of Bosnia and Herzegovina, for the assassination. Bosnia and

Herzegovina was part of the Austrian empire, but some of its citizens

were Serbs. Serbia had won its independence from the Ottoman

Empire just a few decades before. It then fought two wars to gain

land and influence in the Balkans. Serbia and some Bosnian Serbs

now sought to destroy Austria's rule in Bosnia and Herzegovina.

Serbian leaders denied any role in the killing, although one of

their army colonels had armed the killer, 19-year-old Gavrilo Princip.

Austria's Emperor Franz Joseph, uncle of the dead archduke, also

blamed Russia, which had a formal treaty with Serbia. Russian leader

Tsar Nicholas II and his advisers hoped to weaken Austrian rule in

the region.

Franz Joseph wanted war with Serbia. He said, "The continuance

of this state of things constitutes a constant danger to my house and to

my realm." But going to war with Serbia likely meant taking on Russia

as well. And through treaties, Russia had military ties to France and

Great Britain. Franz Joseph knew his army was too weak to fight so many enemies. He turned to his ally, Germany, for help.

Several German states had been united into one nation less than 50 years before. Germany had become a major power in Europe — feared by the Russians, the French, and the British. Germany had built up its industries and was strengthening its military. Franz Joseph could not win a war unless Germany agreed to help.

Germany's leader, Kaiser Wilhelm II, sent word July 6 that Austria-Hungary could rely on German military aid. With that guarantee, Austria made demands on Serbia. These included cracking down on Serbian groups that opposed Austria. Serbia accepted all but two of the demands — demands that would strip the country of its independence. Austria-Hungary then declared war on Serbia, exactly one month after the assassination.

ONE EMPIRE, MANY GROUPS

The Austro-Hungarian Empire, also called Austria-Hungary, had its roots in lands controlled by the Hapsburgs, a powerful German family. The Austrian branch of the family combined its empire with the kingdom of Hungary in 1867 to create the new, larger empire. Within this vast stretch of Europe were people from many backgrounds. The empire's ethnic groups included Germans, Hungarians, Czechs, Slovaks, Poles, Ukrainians, Serbs, Bosnians, Romanians, Croatians, and Italians. The various religious groups included Protestants, Roman Catholics, Greek Orthodox, Jews, and Muslims. The Hapsburgs let some ethnic groups, such as the Hungarians and Croats, have some political freedoms, but others wanted the same freedoms.

GERMANY AT WAR

Germany declared war on Russia on August 1, and two days later declared war on France, a nation bound by treaty to aid Russia. Meanwhile, the Germans signed a secret treaty with the Ottoman Empire, which included what are now Turkey, Iraq, and Syria. The Ottomans agreed to help Germany in a war against Russia. Germany, the Ottoman Empire, and Austria-Hungary would be known as the Central Powers. The war would pit cousins against each other—Kaiser Wilhelm II and England's King George V were grandsons of England's former queen, Victoria. And Tsar Nicholas II was their cousin.

In Vienna, the capital of Austria, some people celebrated when they heard war was at hand. They were eager to punish Serbia for the assassination of the archduke. Some Germans also welcomed a major European war. They saw it as a way to prove Germany's strength. Kaiser Wilhelm II also believed that France, Russia, and Great Britain, called the Triple Entente, wanted to destroy his country because they feared its growing power. Germany had to fight, and win, to survive.

Within the first week of August, more than 3 million German men began preparing for battle. About 840,000 were in the regular army. Others were called into service, and still others volunteered, eager to show their patriotism and bravery. Many German women also pledged their support, ready to serve as nurses or take jobs formerly held by men. With the people behind the war and the country's military strength, German leaders were sure the Central Powers could win a quick victory.

Germany had expected to fight a war on two fronts—against France in the west and Russia in the east. Its troops began heading in both directions. Forces from Austria-Hungary prepared to enter Serbia. Troops would also head east to fight the Russians. Germany's plan was to keep a small force in the east to fight the Russians while focusing most of its forces on a lightning-fast invasion of France.

To do that German troops would have to first march through Belgium and Luxembourg. On August 2, even before declaring war on France, Germany invaded neutral Luxembourg to seize control of the nation's railways. It would need those tracks to move German troops and supplies into France.

Belgium, like Luxembourg, was a neutral country, and Germany had promised not to invade it. Germany demanded the use of Belgium's railways and for Belgium to allow German troops to enter the country. German leaders warned the Belgians that if their troops resisted, Germany would attack. The Belgians did resist, and soon fighting broke out.

The German army used huge siege guns against the Belgians in 1914.

Germany's invasion of neutral Belgium upset Britain. British leaders had warned the kaiser they would declare war if German forces entered Belgium. With the German invasion, all three nations of the Triple Entente were at war with Germany. Those three nations and the countries that joined them in the war against the Central Powers were called the Allies.

Germany seized control of Belgium's major cities and killed some civilians. By the end of August, most of Belgium was under German control. The British accused Germany of brutality against the Belgians. The Germans said they were just defending themselves against Belgian citizens' attacks. It was later discovered that many of the British accusations were false, reported in the hopes of sparking U.S. support of the Allies. But as the town of Louvain burned, German soldiers fired their guns randomly and taunted the fleeing Belgians. One officer looked at a civilian and said, "The crime is yours"—blaming the Belgians for what was happening.

The Austrians, meanwhile, weren't doing so well with their invasion of Serbia. With some of its troops fighting Russia, the Austro-Hungarian army wasn't strong enough to defeat the Serbs. During an August 17 battle near Serbia's Jadar River, the Austrians suffered 40,000 casualties. The Serbs also captured many of their guns and supplies. Within a few days, the Serbs had forced the Austro-Hungarian army out the country. The Serbs held off another Austrian offensive in December at the Battle of Kolubara. The Central Powers were slowly realizing that this Great War would not end as quickly as they had hoped.

SUCCESSES AND FAILURES

*U*nlike Austria-Hungary's problems with Serbia, the

Germans were having more success on both fronts. In August 1914 the

larger German army forced British and French troops to retreat from

eastern France during the Battles of the Frontiers. On the Eastern

Front the Germans won a huge victory at the Battle of Tannenberg.

The Russians had invaded the East Prussia region of Germany

on August 20. The Russians had more soldiers and artillery. But the

forests and lakes near the town of Tannenberg gave the Germans

defensive barriers and made it hard for the Russians to move troops

and supplies. Meanwhile, the Germans had easier access to railways

to move men and equipment. By the end of August, the Germans

German sharpshooters prepare for action in 1914.

had trapped thousands of Russians in a forest, while others had retreated. The Germans captured 92,000 Russian troops and killed at least 30,000.

In the west, despite his troops' victories, German general Helmuth von Moltke faced some problems. His forces had advanced quickly. Germany was having trouble keeping them supplied. The German army needed hundreds of tons of food every day, as well as millions of pounds of food for their horses. The troops often relied on captured supplies to survive. The German soldiers were also tiring after weeks of heavy fighting. Still, Germany's plan was to keep heading west and capture Paris, the capital of France.

By this time the French had strengthened their defenses around the Marne River, which cuts across northeastern France. Now they were the ones who could use their own railways to move soldiers and supplies. Meanwhile, the Germans had sent troops back to Belgium.

The Battle of the Marne began September 5, with French and British forces attacking the advancing Germans. The Germans eventually gave up about 45 miles (72 kilometers) of ground they had

The bloody Battle of the Marne claimed hundreds of thousands of casualties.

earlier won. General Moltke saw the Battle of the Marne as a huge defeat. The war so far, he told his wife, with its "rivers of blood," left him "often overcome by dread." Kaiser Wilhelm's son, Crown Prince Wilhelm, told an American reporter, "We have lost the war. It will go on for a long time, but lost it is already." The kaiser, however, said that the Central Powers would still crush their enemies.

In the field German officers had to come up with their next plan. Moltke ordered his men to retreat to the Aisne River in northeastern France. He told them to dig in and prepare to defend their ground. His order led to what became known as trench warfare—both sides positioned in trenches in the ground, with neither side able to force the enemy out.

Despite the defeat at the Marne, Germany still controlled most of Belgium and a part of France that produced important resources, such as coal and iron. The Allies would have to attack well-defended German forces if they wanted to recapture the land they had lost.

SEA AND AIR BATTLES

While the fighting on the Western Front settled into trench warfare, the Great War was extending to the world's seas. Great Britain carried out a naval blockade. Its ships patrolled the North Sea and English Channel. They stopped ships from bringing food and war supplies to the Central Powers.

Great Britain had the world's largest navy. When it came time to challenge the blockade, the Germans turned to a relatively new weapon—the submarine, known in Germany as the U-boat. In February 1915 the Germans declared the waters around Great Britain a war zone. Any ship entering the zone faced a U-boat attack. Germany tested this declaration May 7, when a German submarine fired a torpedo at the British passenger ship *Lusitania* off Ireland's coast. The ship sank, killing nearly 1,200 passengers and crew. Germany said it was justified in its action because the ship was carrying war supplies to Britain.

The Germans also took the war to Great Britain by air. Airplanes were new weapons—the first successful air flight had taken place in 1903. Early in the war, the Germans had sent airships called zeppelins to bomb Allied cities in Europe. The zeppelins were filled with hydrogen, a gas that is lighter than air. Later the Germans developed bomber planes to carry out that mission. The Germans, like the Allies, also used planes over the battlefields. The best-known German pilot was Manfred von Richthofen, who shot down 80 enemy planes. Often flying a red plane, he earned the nickname "the Red Baron." Richthofen was killed in action in April 1918.

A BIGGER WAR

The Central Powers saw both gains and setbacks through 1915. In April at Ypres, Belgium, the Germans used a poisonous gas, chlorine, as a weapon. They used other harmful gases, including mustard gas, later in the war.

German soldiers opened steel tanks to release the chlorine, which drifted over French troops in their trenches. The gas stung the men's eyes and throat, then filled their lungs with pain. The victims coughed and gasped for air as their skin turned a shade of yellowish green. The unlucky ones died as their lungs shut down. The first German gas attacks killed about 5,000 men. The Germans hoped the gas would give them an advantage over the enemy. The French retreated, but gas that remained in the air kept the Germans from advancing. As the fighting continued, the Germans gained some ground, although they could not drive the Allies out of Ypres.

In the Balkans Austria-Hungary hadn't yet defeated Serbia, so Germany sent troops to help do the job. The Turks were facing a major Allied offensive at Gallipoli Peninsula. The British, along with forces from Australia, New Zealand, and France, had landed there in April 1915.

The Central Powers invaded Serbia in October. Bulgaria had now joined the Central Powers, hoping to weaken Russian influence in the Balkans. By the end of 1915, the Central Powers defeated Serbia.

Before this victory the Turks had stopped Allied offensives around Gallipoli, while also fighting the Russians in a region called the Caucasus. And fighting had opened on a new front, between Austria-Hungary and Italy. The Italians had joined the Allies in

Austrian soldiers aim their machine guns at Italian troops in the Alps.

April 1915. The Austrians and Italians began to fight a series of
battles along the mountainous border between Italy and the empire.

Despite their successes, the Central Powers still faced the
horrors of trench warfare along the Western Front. German soldiers
lived in a series of trenches, often lined with sandbags or wood.
Conditions were horrible. Huge rats ran through the trenches,
insects swarmed, and the air was often filled with the smell of
human waste and dead bodies. By 1916 the Central Powers had
built almost 12,000 miles (19,300 km) of trenches on the battlefields
of Europe. As the trench warfare went on, the Germans built
tunnels to link the trenches, and some men lived as much as 50 feet
(15 meters) below ground. Barbed wire guarded the trenches, and
attacks usually came at night. Artillery boomed and poison gas
filled the air before one side or the other tried to advance. But major
victories were hard to win on the Western Front, with both sides so
well defended in their trenches. The war dragged on.

THE WAR GETS TOUGH

For weeks the Germans prepared for a major assault on the Western Front. General Erich von Falkenhayn now commanded German forces in the west. He wanted to break the will of French citizens to keep fighting, thinking he could convince them "in a military sense they have nothing more to hope for." He chose the city of Verdun as his target. About 7 a.m. February 21, 1916, German artillery roared into action. Their shells sailed 20 miles (32 km) to strike their targets. The Battle of Verdun had begun.

When the shelling stopped about nine hours later, German infantry poured out of their trenches and began to advance. Some used flamethrowers. Gases forced a stream of oil through a tube,

German artillery fires on French forces during the Battle of Verdun.

and the oil was lit just before it sprayed out. The fire usually didn't kill the enemy, but it made them run from their trenches — making them easy targets for German gunners.

At Verdun, after some initial success, the German advance slowed. By March the two sides were fighting a war of attrition. Each side tried to wear down the other and destroy its will to fight. The Battle of Verdun dragged on until December 18 — the longest battle of the war. The Germans gained almost no ground and suffered 337,000 casualties, almost as many as the French. The Germans would not launch another major offensive in the west for more than a year.

Austria-Hungary faced difficult times as well. Russia attacked in the east in March, but the Central Powers beat them back. A second offensive came in June. This time the Russians struck at Austrian forces spread out in trenches along the front in Galicia, in what is now Poland and Ukraine. Surprised by the attack, several hundred thousand Austro-Hungarian troops surrendered. The Russians quickly gained ground. Only the arrival of German and Austro-Hungarian reinforcements later in the summer stopped the enemy's advance.

A horse-drawn mobile soup kitchen helped feed the starving Germans.

PROBLEMS AT HOME

The long, painful war was also affecting the civilians of the Central Powers. In Vienna, many public buildings went without heat or light to save fuel for the military. As meat supplies ran low in parts of Austria-Hungary, horses were slaughtered for food.

Germans also faced food shortages. In the capital of Berlin, anger over shortages and high prices led to protests. Often women led these protests, since so many men were off fighting the war. By 1916 the food shortages were leading to health problems for many Berliners. Going into 1917 Germans experienced what they called the "turnip winter." Many people relied on turnips as their main source of food.

Protests were also sparked by politics. Some Germans were socialists who supported the rights of workers and wanted to end the rule of the kaiser. Socialists opposed the war and thought it benefited the rich. On May 1, 1916, German socialists Rosa Luxemburg and Karl Liebknecht led protests against the war in Berlin. Liebknecht was arrested, and the socialists organized strikes. Tens of thousands of Germans refused to work to protest the arrest.

FACING NEW THREATS

The Russians and French made up the largest land forces the Central Powers faced. The British, though, were the driving force behind several new offensives. One was against the Turks, as the British aided Arabs fighting the Ottoman Empire. On the Western Front, the British led an attack against the Germans along the Somme River.

The battle began in late June, as the British bombarded the German trenches with artillery shells. Men watched their friends die and wondered how long the shelling would go on. As a German private named Eversmann recalled, there was the sense of dread about what was to come: "When will they attack—tomorrow or the day after? Who knows?" The British attack on the German lines began July 1. German machine guns mowed down the advancing enemy soldiers, and the British suffered nearly 60,000 casualties in just that day. The fighting would go on for almost five months. In the end, the British and French gained only about 5 miles (8 km) of land. To defend their position, the Germans suffered about 500,000 casualties.

AT SEA AND OVERSEAS

By the end of 1916, Germany had two new military commanders, Field Marshal Paul von Hindenburg and General Erich Ludendorff. Starting in 1917, they began pulling back some of their troops along the Western Front to a new defensive line, the Siegfried Line, known to the world as the Hindenburg Line. The trenches that made up this line ran from the North Sea south to Pont-a-Mousson, France. The new line was easier to defend than the previous ones.

Germany also made a major change in its sea warfare. It had stepped up U-boat attacks through 1916. In January 1917 the German navy announced that its subs would once again attack ships, both enemy and neutral, that entered the waters around Great Britain.

Kaiser Wilhelm II (center) with his commanders, Paul von Hindenburg (left)
and Erich Ludendorff

ARMENIAN GENOCIDE

The Ottoman Empire's war against Russia led to tragedy for the empire's Armenian residents. Armenians in the Caucasus wanted their own homeland. The empire's Turkish rulers used the war as an excuse to kill Armenians or drive them out of their traditional lands and into Syria, to the south. Along this forced march, Turkish troops killed some Armenians. Others died from starvation, thirst, and disease. As many as 1.5 million Armenians died because of Turkish actions. This is known today as the Armenian genocide—the attempt to wipe out an entire people.

By this time Germany was seeking new allies, in case the Americans entered the war. German Foreign Minister Arthur Zimmermann sent a coded telegram to Heinrich von Eckardt, the German ambassador to Mexico. In it he said that if the United States joined the Allies, Germany would help Mexico regain land it had previously lost to the United States in return for Mexico joining the Central Powers. U.S. President Woodrow Wilson learned about this offer. The news, along with Germany's sinking of U.S. ships, finally brought the United States into the war in April 1917. Germany would have a new enemy to face in the months ahead.

THE ROAD TO DEFEAT
CH. 4

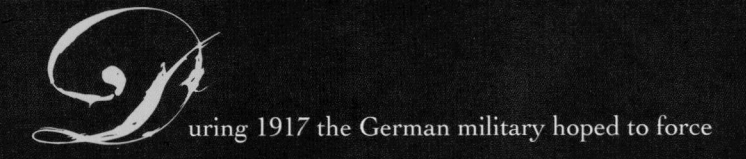

During 1917 the German military hoped to force

Britain's hand with increased U-boat attacks on ships bound for

Britain. But the British were prepared to fight on, and they and the

French launched another offensive that began in April. Fighting

also broke out again around Ypres, Belgium, in July. In both

places the Germans were once again able to keep the enemy from

capturing much territory, though they paid a high price. In fighting

along the Aisne River, the Germans had 168,000 casualties, and at

Ypres the number was 260,000.

German storm troopers emerge from a thick cloud of poison gas.

Events in Russia also helped the Central Powers. Earlier in 1917 the Russians had forced their ruler, Nicholas II, from power. In November socialists called Bolsheviks seized control of the new government. The new Russian government signed an armistice to end the fighting between Russia and Germany. A peace treaty would soon follow. German leaders hoped that the absence of a major Allied nation would turn the tide of the war in their favor.

With Russia out of the war, Germany could move most of its eastern troops to the west. Von Hindenburg and Ludendorff then began to plan a last major offensive against the French and British. They wanted to strike before the major U.S. force arrived in Europe.

The plan was to defeat the British first, along the northern sections of the Western Front around the Somme. Ludendorff counted on small groups of his best soldiers, called storm troopers,

to break through holes in the lines and attack the enemy from behind. He said he was prepared to lose 1 million men in this last great effort to win the war. Ludendorff also realized that new offensives still might not be enough to bring victory. But when peace came, he wanted Germany to control as much land as possible.

WARTIME SUFFERING

As the Germans planned for this assault, the Central Powers entered 1918 as a weak fighting force. Food and natural resources were in short supply. For several years German civilians had been eating ersatz (substitute) food. Coffee was made from barley or dandelion roots. Fake meat was made from flour and mushrooms. In both Germany and Austria, children died in large numbers. More and more German workers went on strike, tired of how they had

Starving Berliners dig through garbage piles looking for food in 1918.

THE HINDENBURG LINE

The Germans began building the Hindenburg Line in 1916. This huge defense system covered nearly 100 miles (160 km) of the Western Front. It was a series of strongholds linked by deep, wide trenches and tunnels and protected by thick belts of barbed wire. Each stronghold held bunkers, which are protected defensive positions, and machine-gun nests made of concrete. As the Germans withdrew to the Hindenburg Line, they flattened everything in front of it so that attackers would have no cover. The Germans believed that the Hindenburg Line was so strong that no army would ever get past it.

suffered during the war. By February Kaiser Wilhelm II realized how his people were hurting. He wanted peace, but he wanted it to come with a German victory. He believed von Hindenburg and Ludendorff's plan would bring that triumph.

The first offensive began in March, near the Somme. The Germans called it Operation Michael, named for Germany's patron saint. The Germans' massive force greatly outnumbered the opposing British troops. The Germans quickly took back some of the ground they had once held. Over the next few months, they launched new attacks and advanced farther into France. But along the way, they suffered high casualties, which included many of the fierce storm troopers. Germany saw what the future held, as more and

more American troops reached France and entered the battle. By September the Allies had begun to punch through the Hindenburg Line, taking land that Germany had held for four years. Austria-Hungary was struggling too, as the Italians began a successful offensive. The Ottoman Empire was becoming less willing to help the other Central Powers. It was more concerned with defending its interests than in helping Germany. On the battlefield, some German troops deserted. Ludendorff still dreamed of more military success, but many Germans were tired of war. So were millions of others in Europe and Asia.

An Allied officer leads his soldiers out of the trenches amidst German shelling.

A convoy of German soldiers heads to the front in 1918.

REVOLUTION AND PEACE

At the end of September, Bulgaria asked the Allies for an armistice. On October 30 Turkey signed an armistice as well, followed four days later by Austria-Hungary.

As their allies sought to end the war, more Germans spoke out against it. Such talk upset German soldiers along the front, who wanted peace only if it didn't weaken their homeland.

But in the German port of Kiel, sailors refused orders to take their ships to sea. Civilians struggled with continuing food shortages and a new menace—a deadly strain of influenza. The "Spanish flu" struck soldiers too. German socialists stepped up calls for strikes and prepared for a revolution. The government began

to give elected lawmakers more power, but Kaiser Wilhelm II refused to step down. But as protests grew and a revolution broke out, German generals could no longer support the kaiser. It was announced November 9 that Wilhelm was giving up his throne.

Two days later the guns fell silent on the Western Front. Germany had signed an armistice with the Allies. The terms of the agreement said Germany had to give up tens of thousands of weapons and all of its submarines. The Allied blockade would continue. The armistice was just the first step in ending the war. Next would come peace treaties. The Allies wanted a separate one with each defeated Central Power.

In 1919 the Allies met in Paris to write the treaty. The Germans had no say in the details. The final Treaty of Versailles, signed June 28, 1919, angered many Germans. The British and French wanted them to pay a high price for the war. Germany had to accept full responsibility for starting the war and had to pay reparations— money to help the Allies rebuild what the war had destroyed. The treaty also forced Germany to drastically reduce its military and give up its air force. Germany had to give land to France and the newly formed nation of Poland. For Austria-Hungary and the Ottoman Empire, the war meant the end of their empires. Newly independent states were carved out of Austria-Hungary. The Turks gave up large chunks of land to the British and French.

The peace treaty upset Germans for many reasons. They thought it was wrong to blame them alone for starting the war. And they could never pay the reparations the Allies demanded—they were

simply too high for a country that had been so weakened by war. Some Germans also believed that their army could have won the war. They said socialists and others who opposed the war had betrayed the German military.

In Germany, anger over the way World War I ended did not fade. A politician named Adolf Hitler was able to use that anger to help win control of Germany. During the 1930s he illegally rebuilt the German military and then launched World War II. A killing in Sarajevo in 1914 started a chain of events that shaped history through most of the 20th century.

A protest led by Adolf Hitler in 1933 against the Treaty of Versailles would eventually lead to another devastating conflict, World War II.

INDEX